Where there is Hope

Shafina Khatun

Presentation by *BookLeaf Publishing*

Web: www.bookleafpub.com

E-mail: info@bookleafpub.com

ISBN: 9789357212298

First edition 2023

A Nightingale's melody

You were sent to me in a dream
At first it was the gentle hum
Of a Nightingale's melody

I searched through the lands
Following the sweet sorrow
Of a Nightingale's melody

My heart longed for you
As I heard the ache
Of a Nightingale's melody

Until I was lead into the dark
and there was no more
of a Nightingale's melody

but I arrived to a place
where the moon shone bright
and the melody brought me to you

A Parrots strength

2

Her frail hands tell a story of great care
She nursed each feather with happiness
As her Parrot stared at her with great love
He chose his words carefully as he stared on
Both in silence wondering in great thought
His colourful wings spread apart to set off
As he took to the sky with great strength

The Peacock descends paradise

A princess cried her self to sleep every night
So He took pity and send down in flight
One of his most beautiful Peacocks to protect
Over this young girl so they could both connect
The Peacock transformed as he ascended down
Becoming a strong handsome man as he hit the
ground
He was approached by a royal guard who said
'do you want work in exchange for your daily
bread?
We have a task' the foul guard began to whisper
And when he finally finished handed a dagger
Which the young man took and nodded his head
Off he went silently looking for the Princesses
bed

The Peacock tells the truth

Now he understood why he had been sent from
paradise
He found her asleep in a troubled state and
began to memorize
Her every facial feature so he could immortalise
The state of her beauty so unreal, he had always
empathised
But he slowly awakened her and she leapt in
surprise
He told her everything, the truth uttering no lies
Her eyes still wide in shock said 'you're finally
here
The King has died and my Step-mom has me in
fear
I am to marry a man of my wishes but every
night
I cry to sleep as she sends assassins to snuff my
light
But they are unable to do so because of this
chain'
Amulet of a Peacock made them drop dead in
pain
'only my true Prince a watcher of royalty
Would not be affected and be able to set me free
From my cruel Step-mom's evil plan'
He realised why he had been sent down as a man

The Peacock becomes a King

5

The following day the Step-mom waited on her
seat
She stared at the throne trying to attain it was no
mean feat
The doors opened and in walked the princess
arm in arm
With none other than the young man the guard
hoped would harm
The very young Princess now held in a loving
embrace
Who now turned to the court with immense
grace
The protection has been lifted and now we have
a King
Open the court window so the birds may sing
Of the tale of a bird of paradise sent to save this
mortal princess
Oh Step-mom tell no lies for you must confess
How you had been sending assassins every night
to me
But they were unsuccessful and now from your
hold I am free'
So the Step-mom confessed and was banished
away

The Raven's disguise

Calamity came in the form of a disguise
A raven perched on my window
Dooming my life from this moment on
My crops began to die from severe drought
A bad omen came my way, I wept and I cried
I prayed and I prayed but the tears never stopped
And still this Raven stayed perched watching my tears
I quietened my cries and spoke softly to this bird
Then at the stroke of midnight when I cried no more
Gentle drops hit my roof I rushed to the window
And saw the rain cascading down on the lands
As the Raven flew off into the sky I finally understood
He had been a blessing wrapped in hardship

The Eagle's bravery

7

I trembled on the branch with my wings huddled
to me
Too afraid to take a new journey and cross the
endless sea
But the water below showed a bold Eagle to be
my reflection
So I spread my wings and became my fearless
transformation

The Owl's barn

A small Owl hid in an abandoned barn lost from
her family
A thunderous rain had uprooted them of their
blanket security
As she looked at the barn window and saw her
reflection
She wondered where her family were whilst she
lived in seclusion
Before being startled by a tap she had wanted to
cry at her misfortune
Surprised to see from the window was a smiling
red-breasted robin

Robin's hope

'Oh Owl you are the few blessed of wisdom
cloaked in mystery
You cry when deep insight is your profound
ability
Come to me and whisper your pain in my ear
Oh dear, how did you lose your family in this
vast sphere?
Well until we find them you are my friend,
family and companion
I will give you hope of a new day until the day
you all meet in reunion'

The Magpies logic and the Swans love

The Magpie perched mighty and tall on the
branch of the riverbank tree
Looking down on the swan floating in the water
elegantly
'I am better than you for I represent logic,
intellect and brain',
Magpie said ,'whilst you ponder around living in
nothing but vain'
'you may lead to a certain extent with the use of
your intellect'
Replied Swan 'but why must you and I endure
such conflict?
Logic is to you what emotion is to me, my
passion emits light
You're perched on your branch but you still
haven't attained full height
Look at the space underneath where no branches
can dwell
We must respect each others way so we can live
in parallel

The grim Vulture

A Vulture saw a small family of owls washed
ashore
Still, dead they looked to be breathing no more
Whilst a young owl and red-breasted robin stood
with tears
No family, all alone, young Owl was swallowed
by fear
But Vulture thought was this world not meant to
break ones heart?
Or do the attached fail to realise we shall one
day depart
 Aren't we strangers of the land, our footsteps
temporary?
So why pain over a breathe in a world that's not
eternity?

The Hawk of Omar

People would tell the tales of the enlightened
man Omar
His elegant Hawk would remain perched on his
shoulder
Inspiringly he'd say, 'each of you have a secret
to discover
Like those who searched the heavens and they
began to uncover
The magic from astrology to give us the science
of astronomy
Or foolish gold-making alchemists who gave us
chemistry
So do not limit yourself noble people listen to
my word
Don't hold yourself back you can all be
enlightened like my bird

Mockingbird's innocence

13

Her spirit was pure and innocent
Was the gravest sin to take her life
Her tiny life bought joy to all around
So who were you to take that away
And now she haunts you in your dreams

Bat's rebirth

I'm in a dark place
I can't breathe and I can't see
With every second
My life flashes before me
Oh dear mother earth
How do I hurt so badly
I am weak and frail
I'm not ready for rebirth
'Dear Bat you will be fine'
Said mother earth
'Trust in me and my power
Some I gave the light
But to you I gave the dark
Open your true sight
And you will be guided'

Duck's conscience

15

I'm torn between what society wants
And what I truly want to be
You see me like a Duck afloat on water
But under water is where my secret lies
Do not throw me the bread
For you do not know what I need
You may think you are feeding me
But really you don't know what is best
You are constricted by your narrow mind
Let you be you and let Duck be a Duck

Athena's patridge

16

I stood by the great goddess Athena
And so too helped birth a nation
For though She was the goddess of symbol
I live on as her mighty servant
So where you cannot find Athena
Know I am a mere flight away

Heron's balance

I could not balance my life
It was tattered and in pieces
Until I watched her in awe
Stood on one leg for hours
She turned to me and said
'what I do requires patience
Do not be in awe of me
What you see is days,
Weeks, months and years
Of painful tiresome practice
Which now I make effortless
Do not give up on your own path
To find stability and balance'

Finch's sweet sorrow

How could you make me sing
How could you call me Finch
Only to turn your back on me
A bird trapped but should be free
How could you make me love you
Making me weak vulnerable to you?
But this small bird will still be happy
For she knows life is about adaptability

True Freedom

Whenever you see us fly
Up in the heavenly sky
Marvel in awe at our freedom
And how we travel the dominion
With the wings as our blessings
But for you to travel our dwelling
You need man-made flight
To really attain such height
So respect and cherish us all
Mighty big to mighty small